PEACE, POWER AND LOVE

MR. JOEL WASHINGTON ATTERBURY

King Atterberry Ink

Copyrighted © 2021 Library of Congress.

Published by: JOEL WASHINGTON ATTERBURY
King atterberry 9

ISBN: 978-1-7352952-7-5

Contact Information
Email: kingatterberry7@gmail.com
Facebook: Joel Washington Atterbury
Instagram: king_atterberry7
Instagram: king_atterberry_ink
Photographed submitted by

TABLE OF CONTENTS

Acknowledgement

This book dedicated to two men who have been instrumental in my life, with me gaining knowledge of self.

Crazy thing about it is that they shared the same birthday.

MY BROTHER

Mr. Prescott Harris aka Mystic Mind always held an open door to his library of literature for me to indulge in.

Musically and creatively my brother allowed me to see and hear what was happening in the arts of the world.

As his younger brother it's been a wonderful experience learning from him how to maneuver in this world ever since I was a youth.

Much power and respect to my older brother love you.

BEST FRIEND

Mr. Robert knight aka freedom jalah one of my best friends who I loved as if he was my own biological brother.

Always will I carry my brother's spirit with me, though he is not here on this plane of existence.

He will always and forever be known for building with me on levels about life and what you see inside yourself.

Besides, he would say to me PEACE and POWER GOD do you know today's mathematics I would say no, and he would be like here let me break it down to you.

And to me that was peace with living in south jersey and he is bringing them lessons to me from a New York state of mind.

Sleep in peace my brother

Someone to love

When you believe in the heart that make you feel the truth.

The will and testament of God will give you the proof.

Any decision made don't be afraid of what they say.

Just know that you are great in many different ways.

Troubled souls find healing after the merge of a purge.

We all want to be heard and not served like hors d'oeuvres.

As the lines become blurred due to bad connectivity.

There's a bright distinguished light check around the vicinity.

Feel vibes that are alive through a frequency that's high.

All spells are not dry wait for the tears when angels cry.

It's the rain that's plain cover your pain with no blame.

Accept the change that's on the ledge of gods window pain.

We grow up and try to make sense of what our eyes see.

But at the same time there is a struggle we don't see.

How man and women supposed to be true inside of belief.

Many times, we drift free and miss blessed deliveries.

Love, care, and respect treasure the loyalty of honesty.

Escape the fools of comedy express and show modesty.

Cool, calm, and collective invest on new prospective.

Don't lose life lessons there's an angel with a message.

Prepare for the happenings coming to your life.

Never doubt what's in your route to make you feel nice.

Two spots of warmth

Our feelings are the same nothing is ever
gonna change.

We are bonded by the heart mind and soul let
me explain.

That special place of space that we share and
hold dear.

Sparks fly when we are close and near
sharing our air.

No situationship only time when the
clock tick.

Taking a trip through her eyes reaching her
inner compartment.

Expectancy is not on the table when
we're together.

Enjoy the intimate moments flashing
memories as lovers.

I am man all day shifting her ways
as we play.

Intimate playmates becoming more than
what we say.

Yet on the real she loves the touch and the
hug I'm her crush.

Kiss her lips and her neck until she blushes
from hot stuff.

Moving herself closer to the closure starting
my motor.

I'm also the one who told her that I'm
stationed like a soldier.

No price is right we wheel of fortune
for the night.

Temporarily in her life as if snake eyes
on the dice.

Good-bye baby

You ask me to understand but your mind
seem distracted.

Performing as if you came in my life
as an actress.

In a new role with a new soul that haven't
found yourself.

Had to let my heart sing a song please find
some help.

Seems to me your confusion was infused
with conflicting.

Strange decisions based on your poor
choices of living.

Absentee of compassion and care
you disappeared.

Threw our love elsewhere move your
rear to next gear.

My driving point on the gps is less stress.

I already passed God test also I wish
you the best.

No longer hear your hello or see a greeting through text.

I'm peaceful upon my mental rest starting my quest.

Never thought you'd be another women lost in a mess.

When you mess up your lucks up can't even recognize the best.

Why should I be mindful and thoughtful you deserve you?

I'm on the good foot to continue checking out the world menu.

A1

I don't need an original only rock
with imperials.

My drive on life captured with GOD on the
steering wheel.

Hang time moment shots of brown
liquor thinking.

Corona virus thoughts corona one
lemon drinking.

Sitting in a lounge with nice music
and women.

Dressed in a button up shirt my jeans
blue denim.

Personally, I'm chilling inside the
vibes of auras.

Talk glass of water with a straw calling
my daughter.

Wondering about life and how the
world be turning.

Society on fire children of darkness
walking and burning.

Soul searching for peace once released
from a vessel.

Outsiders speaking blasphemy and
trying to catch you.

Emotions of the righteous call on the
lord to fight this.

That's why I joined the writers and spoken
word reciters.

Send a message to society one day
accept sobriety.

Until then admire me I'm never
where the liars be.

I'm wireless tired of this Ill-mannered
craziness.

Dissolve bad relationships escape
on gods' graciousness.

Pour water on my face say a prayer
after my morning.

My spirit felt a warning that a new
wave is forming.

NEW ONE, TWO

Last time king was seen in a poetry
corner scene.

Spitting a rhyme scheme across a
Facebook screen.

Went back to old ways check the
strength of my page.

This year I have plenty to say a
new day of age.

Can't cage a lion y'all need to stop trying.

Turn into a swordsman with bars
sharp as iron.

Aging backwards through
meditation and prayer.

Only reason I wear a crown because
I was the next heir.

Dad passed away young, so it was
passed to his son.

I was an underdog child born on the first of
the eighth month.

Study lessons aggressive mentally stayed humble.

Got schooled about life so big thanks to my uncle.

So, peace to Les the best I found a new wooden chest.

Open the treasured box see what's next on the bless.

If its all in the cards, then it's all from the stars.

What is parked next to ours wasn't part of a level marked.

Incredible lift!

Signs of new beginnings change
months of arrival.

Allow spirit to drive through pathways
of survival.

Display new array of something special
within self.

Feelings that are felt on the waist
without a belt.

Standing inside of a place where all
had failed.

Move waves of motivation inspired by
held scales.

Statue of a fool been replaced by a new cool.

Keeping the heart youthful with a
beautiful attitude.

Distinctive look on life is very nice
for the soul.

God given code opening a gold road.

Treasure map so unique telepathic
upon the reach.

Gifting the one who speak in a language
that's tai chi.

Richness is the blessing of
manifesting goals.

Regaining all control of what was lost
switching modes.

Forever friendly creator the one who sent me.

Even at half century emotions I move quickly.

Worthy

Travel to a place where I am reintroduced.

Excited about a muse that found
my old attribute.

Abdul Haleem salaam was my name before
my name.

King is who I be now since the new
wave came.

In a world that's so strange society
need to change.

No blame no shame I exist on both planes.

Don't check my spirituality worry
about your reality.

So many where the cattle be that's why
I'm sucker free.

Walk around favors as if I'm greeted by
nosey neighbors.

Eye raise on traitors same as I do to
the haters.

Silence is golden just smile and
keep it moving.

Why should I be proving points to those
already losing?

Step up ladders to progress remain
strong and modest.

Leave summer inside of august while
some stay out of pocket.

Shoot for the stars with these bars
already charged.

Resonate on moons while y'all play
around with Mars.

Lord knows!

Mercy me living free raising my hands
unto the sky.

Pillar point to which I rise holding
heaven in my eyes.

Never one to look back after I spoke
with the most high.

Express the reason and told me let
it go inside.

So, I took them words in and started
praying more often.

Regulated my reading to being
scheduled instead of portioned.

Cradled the scriptures examined the
lines now it's God time.

Lifting my sight beyond all the signs
building a way to search and find.

Group of folks that can feel the love of
nature existing in its living.

Stop forgetting about the man, woman,
and children outside of prisms.

Laws of attraction seat to the soul all on the same timeline.

When the heart shine with an open mind all is done through humankind.

Hands loose

Walking down blocks bend a corner
take a hike.

Reach top of hill and chill make sure
traffic is right.

Before I cross street that's flooded high step
the pavement.

Full view amazing catches up with friends
that are playing.

Tunes of a time when music fed the
heart with joy.

The barbecue is real and the
energy non-void.

Hands holding plates of food and beverages.

Wonderful the time expressing togetherness.

Couch conversations laughter is in the air.

Small groups dancing bodies
moving everywhere.

Others singing along to the songs by
many singers.

Smoke passed around to a few nondrinkers.

Memories of peace and pleasurable
guest interacting.

Partying like it's Vegas where
anything can happen.

All adult event it's a nice cool gathering.

Cell phones catching lovely shots
as folks scattering.

Beneficial

When my eyes close and there's no more me.

Forget my books of poetry there's a new I.D.

Abdul-Haleem salaam woke up early
this morning.

A storm just came through take heed to
the warning.

Lightning so bright striking clouds
that's dark grey.

Feel like 1999 true indeed it's Cape May.

Representative I'm on that old Harlem flip.

Be careful what you are talking about check
how the GOD get.

Remote control intuition shifting the
laws of physics.

Grinding so hard from a fresh start to finish.

Let me manage my business matter fact stay
out my business.

Back smoking that green with a six
pack of Guinness.

Why should I lay low in a
population controlled?

Brighten my glow and upload a
fresh download.

Touch matters in ways that have me say
what I say.

Remain brave even when they wanna throw
me away.

IM BACK!

Double lane exchange

Behind the wall I draw four and plan
more to score.

Gym bag packed on the floor against the
white wall.

When I make my escape out of
state and visit.

A trip so exquisite this open flight can't
miss it.

Copped the rental from enterprise this
is no pop up.

Verbal Invitation made when I arrive that's
what's up.

Itinerary unplanned it's a go with
the flow moment.

Right now, I'm just vibing with an outer
earth zoning.

Nothing ever bizarre I don't walk
inside mirages.

Relaxed watching the stars hearing jimmy
hen guitars.

Sound of this occasion patient
while I'm waiting.

A week off from work celebrating
my new vacation.

Unpack my flyers and books, cards,
and notes.

My time built with hope and faith
covering gross.

Steal a few beautiful days from out the week.

Formulate my meet and greet outside in
public streets.

What it do!

Stay inside the ways that I have I'm just me.

Arriving in high degrees so I live easily.

Some wonder how I breathe and exist.

I don't move from a standing point only walk
inside of shifts.

Mood is always steady I am
different Atterbury.

Not much weight to carry swim
outside of many levies.

Ride tides of mayhem adapt to any chaos.

Dressed is colored rayon open
bright prayers.

Who are the outsiders examining God flyers?

Report to your messiah that the guard
became higher.

Leave a post of choice without
opening voice.

Let's shut down the noise and call
up the boys.

Team keeping dreams format the
broke moral.

Switching up a style unheard of for a while.

Let's flip the unnatural doing what
we have to.

Passing through a truth so beautiful
is how we do.

Believe and receive

Stars illuminated from what the
galaxy created.

Lights of life amazing what a sight
for me naked.

Gazing from a view so in aww
watching its beauty.

Mars precious image is an outer space ruby.

Full moon flashing no caption for
what is coming.

New flirt that works thoughts now running
into something.

Retrograde posted up spiritual
billboard end month.

Don't know what's in front better
understand who won.

Pure natural order within a force
greater than us.

Strange to us is the cusp
transformation of a trust.

Entering a form that's warm
outside the norm.

Make sure you send away from home
and set a better tone.

Experience of knowing who is and who isn't.

May the heart find a tenant lose the
memory of remnants.

Past path never last change route
of all courses.

Resolutions are a coin toss enjoy
what's truly yours.

ILL chill grammar

Only reason I bring it back most of these
acts are whack.

Reciting on hot tracks their lyrics is
pure trash.

Give me time and a half spin around a
whole graph.

Sleep on me you get washed and
drowned by avalanche.

The page become full after the lines get
word played.

There's a lyrical tidal wave coming from
cape May.

Started up in New York the fort of all forts.

Contacted the source and got my
energy import.

Momentum is on a thousand barely under
five yards.

Leave competition in the dark
with a bookmark.

Study the last guardian from a
tribe of wanderers.

Make your mind ponder sweat a
response from my sauna.

Come through as heat wave scorch
flesh like dry ice.

Over here there's nothing nice except a
hand with hot dice.

When I roll them it's like hitting all
pins in bowling.

I'm off the bench with common sense it's a
strike I be knowing.

Gone but not forgotten

She connects with respect therefore I walk
into the next.

Ever since we both met it's been one
helluva catch.

Vibes going crazy it's wavy off the surfboard.

Open door to explore we might be
looking for.

Ok upon the day speak in a language
that play.

Display a mutual appreciation all
I'm gonna say.

Dial up the mental reading notes
off my kindle.

I'm an original only one I
resemble is confidential.

Never one to be carry peace, power,
and structure.

Move around these others its monopoly
Parker brothers.

Complicated risk holistic bracelets
on my wrist.

Ancestral necklace shown I hope that y'all
don't miss.

King is a creator with that little joe flavor.

Unlike my father I write my life on
lined paper.

Game changer where do I go if
they're not ready.

Internalize experience hearing some
many medleys.

Women of words

Your voice so impressive so expressive
with your life.

Fighting against fright with all your might
looking nice.

Beating the odds again remembering him or
even them.

Paying attention to the world that
society's living in.

Enhancing the train of thought while others
lost still searching.

Strong enough to break a burden and know
what is deserving.

You're a queen not a meme that is seen
highly acknowledged.

What is started can be solid at the same time
kept out closets.

Scale percentage balanced its fifty
on the mindset.

Hope and faith honest waiting
haven't arrived yet.

Plant seed of discussion embracing nature's own.

Dialing up love to find the heart a healthy home.

Things that you were used to once was very beautiful.

Make sure that it's suitable and your able to continue.

Capture the essence of belief and be still on broken days.

Be vigilant when you speak and never doubt what you.

Higher me!

Absorb and embrace the change it's a
three piece.

When I release and find peace stay
sharper than a crease.

Energy come and go although I grow
in the fold.

Resurrect an old soul that show exactly
what I know.

Counselor at a camp never a
chump or a champ.

Place literature that hit ya you'll
remember the ant.

Strong and pretty mighty work underneath
the surface.

Always keep my purpose on deck with
open service.

Rest my physical on her thoughts while she
is mining my day.

Forget the offset moments that's lost when
greats date.

Taste the tunes on Spotify that was made to check out.

It's an overnight listening while I lounge on work couch.

Ouch fully awaken there's no mistaken.

Beautiful spirits creating what's up with those hating.

Swim inside the pool that's cool that's what I do.

Who am I losing to my motivation ain't you?

Men of respect

Took a long time to get here so now
I am prepared.

Grab a piece of sunshine and put it in
high gear.

I hear inside my ear feeling vibes in the air.

No need for an encore when I stand on
two cheers.

Always participating stationed while
I'm creating.

Thoughts on full course spiritual navigation.

Ride clouds without crowds I'm here in
the now.

There's no father to my style,
I don't have a style.

Only exist through origins of
hard-working people.

Without motivation could have easily
been evil.

So, when I handshake an image that stand in front of me.

Appropriate greeting now it's back to life delivery.

Grounds of walk killing steppingstones of humility.

Using my ability and drive on those feeling me.

Partner up teams that dream and manifest.

My spirit will never rest until God stop saying yes.

Men of respect pt.2

Make my rounds in various places elevating
the youth.

That's what counselors do activation against
the fools.

Speaking inside the realm of knowing and
not guessing.

Treading on thin water it's a blessing what's
your question.

Unofficial as a teacher my studies was in
the ghetto.

Always the type of fellow kind
cool and mellow.

When around the giants and tyrants
I was defiant.

Joined many alliances wolf tickets
I never buy it.

Discipline of a monk always focusing
on my goals.

The road might be closed I stay in lanes
with no toll.

E-Z Pass my gift until the well running dry.

I'm the type of guy that give any
moment a try.

Once all things are applied house my
myself into others.

Bonding with my sisters and brothers even
the mother's.

Sometimes fathers don't bother until we're at
a higher age.

Collecting from what he made and come
back on better days.

Hidden features

Arms too short to shoot a wicked jump shot.

Build is too weak to accomplish a layup.

Game is handicap to make a play any way.

Tired words displayed might as well
never speak.

Crisis of a brother that lost his backbone.

Lack of confidence is shown with a
head down.

Identity of love and care once was
remembered.

Why even reminisce on a time when
smiles appeared.

Understanding of possibility was
just imaginative.

Caught inside the web of a beauty
that disappeared.

Without recovery mirror reflect an
image so ugly.

Why even lift a spirit that's buried in
blind emotions.

Never be good enough perhaps option a
poor choice.

Allow the darkness to close in and sleep
inside of thoughts.

Praying to God for a transformation
rebuilding the presence.

With scriptures became reborn as a Christian
thankful lesson.

Tides turning wheels of life on standby
check the canvas.

Immortal anguish eyes closed visions of rain.

Replica of the past disappointment
inside the present.

Backyard bedroom sitting on the edge
of the future.

World biggest loser playing around in
many circles.

Deaf dumb and blind curfew change squads
find rehearsals.

Sanctuary falls short of what tomorrow
never bring.

Substitutions without gratitude
congratulations once again

Take it to God!!

Never one to throw scriptures only paint
verbal pictures.

Beware of silent whispers from the same
chick that kiss ya!

Unrighteous lips can send your
mental on a trip.

Have a person forget who exactly
he is involved wit.

Mixed up from emotions her words
spoken through a potion.

Have you unbalanced with your
motion as if you dozing?

Finally awoken from a trance and can't stand.

On your own two without her feeling
like you the man.

Never to understand how the plans
from Lilith work.

Daughter of Lucifer get you stamped
under earth.

Splash your face church water wash the
evil from your soul.

At first, you'll feel cold then gain
back self-control.

Light will shine bright angels saving
your half-life.

Could have died in blind sight without
paying a price.

Thank those who pray for us therefor
we're spared from harm.

Our ancestors are charmed with a
failsafe alarm.

My other brother

Always and forever in my heart mind
and soul.

My brother transitioned and my
emotions became cold.

Can't face the fact he not here in
the physical.

So, to me it's a bad dream that was
spoken uncool.

I don't even wanna believe about
the news I received.

At the same time, I keep my brother's spirit
on my sleeves.

He gave me gladiator knowledge of self
through applications.

Told me what he was facing but left
out some situations.

I never asked but I knew he was on a
crossed path.

Told me why I should be a certain way
and never flash.

Keep a light dim therefore your silent thoughts are low.

Wake up and move about and carry an illuminated glow.

I miss my brother freedom jalah a true shining star.

Peace and power upon his spirit that I will know as BIG PA.

Learned a lot from him he was my daughter's godfather.

So deep inside my mind he will remain there as a charger.

Enter off the exit

Before I die let me enjoy a piece of
mind on a timeline.

Take a trip back to Cali fall in love
with the sunshine.

Hit the beach touch the water with bare feet
in the ocean.

Roll up something good and just ignore
the commotion.

Afterward grab a nice meal to eat and enjoy.

Wine glass filled with compliments from staff
that's employed.

Beautiful choice on the white I'm just
relaxing tonight.

Listen to music by a Latin group the
singers alright.

Bounce back to the spot where I chill
scribe a text.

Unsure of what's next meet up with honey
from the desk.

Half hour before her shift ends its
close to midnight.

Catch an Uber or a Lyft so we can dance
where there's life.

I'm no Travolta but I'm stepping within the
right direction.

Hug and kiss on this connection with
a lot of affection.

Mr. Cool nonchalant no arrogance is
what she wants.

We been talking for about a month, and some
change her name is dawn.

Met her through a relative who travel around
on business.

She into crystals, stones and mischief
bringing all to our spirit.

Special lady gorgeous woman physically
and mentally.

Sent me an email saying that she can't wait
until she meets me.

Untitled SALUTE!

Spit words with no problem write a twelve in twenty minutes.

My sentence carries a vengeance coming from hip hop lineage.

Studied the top three Mel, Caz, and Kool Moe Dee.

Rakim, KRS, daddy Kane and Kool G.

My study hall was a terrace, card table and a box.

Instrumental cassette tapes played on repeat until it stops.

Creating a lot of verses for the purpose of whatever.

Entered ciphers with other writers so I can freestyle better.

Various beats alone lift the mind to many levels.

Fire pit emotions having you spitting lines on devils.

Aura so alive that it survives days in a week.

Style on competition till they flow
become weak.

Joe speaks through a young heart that
match in any era.

A go getter with an arsenal of lyrics
that can measure.

Up to whichever standard manage
skills of craft.

Doubt if I crash when I cross
paths and clash.

Nine by nine

When I forgot to return, I got the
call and a text.

Woke up from sleeping to my relative
much respect.

No need to reminisce on the wrong
our family bond.

Although they were wrong, we both left
alone a song.

So, it's back to the love we both grown
from a mishap.

Watching them make moves and be cool
around the world trap.

Sent them a strong congratulations and
condolences to the past.

Speaking about life having a blast
within a laugh.

Explained about prayers and
meditation lifestyle.

Sent a message to their cloud so they can
understand how.

Practice stillness and beware of the illness.

It's not about the realness it's about
how we feel us.

Struggle enough to maintain inside our
culture to succeed.

There's a crab in every barrel trying to
grab you by your heels.

Swim beyond the points of warning signs
and lean on God.

Finish your business from the start and open
the hidden heart.

Polluted

It's scary outside that's why I stay
inside of self.

Take a weekend off just to adjust
my thoughts.

What's going on, something wrong our
breathing compromised

Strange people everywhere how come
they not prepared.

Perhaps maybe scared of what's
happening in the world.

Open a commonsense grenade so that
we all are aware.

Mixed up emotions holding what the
news reporting.

Poke a hole in that bubble and help the
land with caution.

Free source of information passed
along to others.

Only thing I cover, and deliver is
peace so why suffer.

Gather bodies of those who propose
knowledge of know.

When I author STORY OF LO it's a
different type of intro.

Truth without proof is just a scoop rumored.

Until homework is done, and your antenna
receives a tuner.

Amplified to speakers carry vibes of
many leaders.

Find a seeker to the leader that can find
earth a feeder.

Extreme means

When they call upon the nine, I'm team
justice league.

Find me by the water where it's
easily to breathe.

I'm so aquatic flow outside of tides.

Emerge from the waves when the full
moon shine.

Body start feeling funny from the beacon.

Opposition mad because I'm meeting
with those eating.

Sparks flying across sand when I'm
walking on land.

Tell honey I love her and I'm sorry
I couldn't dance.

Search turfs for answers only
question is who did it?

Last one to visit tried to mimic the
guard mission.

My voltage vision which was given
through creators.

Sharp as gem razors brighter than hot lasers.

Intuition strong enough to sense
from far away.

Reading signs from cross state home-
base is by the bay.

Recalibrate the mind thoughts and
energy a thousand.

Not many can appreciate a beautiful
time of lounging.

Moment of science

Peace to my brothers and sisters
walking, talking life.

Let us all band together and unite on
the real fight.

World is on fire dark clouds crowding
our judgement.

Hold one another in our need and
help a public.

Cease and assist on society that is filled
with many ills.

Memorize the greatest feel until our
hearts build a shield.

Weaponize our brain with survival
tactics against them.

Bring our family and friends into a group
with no system.

Create from the highest the ultimate alliance.

March like a giant waking up from
dead silence.

Speak with strong grammar emphasize what we're saying.

Hug the love with no shrug so we're not playing with our praying.

Only mission I see correct those heads of manipulation.

Bath them in knowledge so they see the whole equation.

Tip the scale of wrong and right the ways of people.

Hoping that I don't hold you or keep you from seeing evil.

Full throttle pt.2

When my pen hit the page there
is no masquerade.

I get straight to the point let's
engage in charade.

Kill all facades they done charged
up the guard.

Finishing what your start I go hard
with my darts.

Ink spilling on paper bring all the
smoke if you want.

Give you punks a captain crunch with a
big Hawaiian Punch.

This verse slam dunk as if it's
all-star weekend.

Never mind what you be speaking
this is a anyone seating.

Bring it and watch me change the
narrative of spitting.

Hit targets from a distance while I
look at you different.

Microphone commander big executing planner.

Strike with lines coming at your head flow hammer.

Hope you enjoy this addition to the

king atterberry ink collection of poetry books.

AUTHOR AND POET KING ATTERBERRY

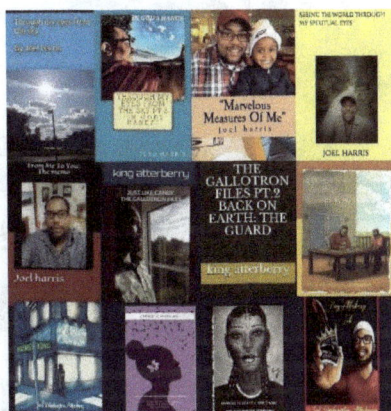

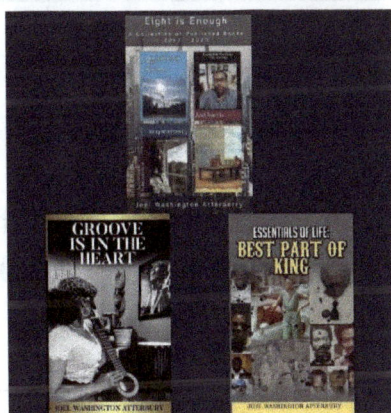

THE POETRY CORNER

HOST

KING ATTERBERRY

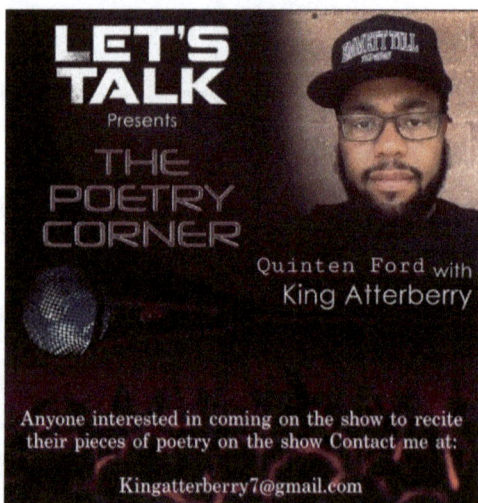

Special thanks to:

Mr. Quinten Ford for keeping the show flowing with drive and determination through great vision.

Anyone interested in donating to help put my books in the hands of those unfortunate to receive them please contact me by email or cashapp donations.

All non-profit

Email me at: **kingatterberry7@gmail.com**

SUPPORT
AUTHOR AND POET
KING ATTERBERRY

THANK YOU
Joel Washington Atterbury
Scan to pay $JoeLTheGuard71

Also scan to purchase books through my linktree

And information to my social media

Joel
Washington
atterbury